Motivational Interviewing in Nutrition and Fitness

The Proven Consulting Approach to Help Clients Overcome Ambivalence, Break Free from Diets and Overcome Barriers to Change

Wendy Robbins

WENDY ROBBINS

Wendy Robbins is a school psychology professor at one of the best schools in Missouri. She was one of the first experts to approach Classroom Check-up, an assessment-based teacher consultation model. Her research focuses on preventing disruptive behavior problems in children and increasing school's implementation of evidence-based practices.

To have a greater impact on people she decided to write her amazing 7 book series called "The Happiness Education Factory".

Wendy Robbins wishes everyone good progress!

Copyright 2021 by Wendy Robbins - All rights reserved.

No part of this publication or the information in it may be quoted from or reproduced in any form by means such as printing, scanning, photocopying or otherwise without prior written permission of the copyright holder.

Disclaimer and Terms of Use: Effort has been made to ensure that the information in this book is accurate and complete, however, the author and the publisher do not warrant the accuracy of the information, text and graphics contained within the book due to the rapidly changing nature of science, research, known and unknown facts and internet.

The Author and the publisher do not hold any responsibility for errors, omissions or contrary interpretation of the subject matter herein. This book is presented solely for motivational and informational purposes only.

Table of Contents

Introduction 9

Chapter 1: A New Approach to Nutrition and Fitness 12

   Motivational Interviewing: What is it? 15

Chapter 2: Current Status of Nutrition and Fitness 17

   Ambivalence 19

   To prevent ambivalence from getting in the way of your nutrition and fitness goals, you may want to ask yourself these questions: 20

      What makes you want to start eating healthier meals and exercising more often? 20

      What are your thoughts about changing your nutrition and fitness behaviours? 21

      How much do you believe these statements about making changes in your nutrition and fitness behaviours? 21

   Beliefs 22

   Motivation 23

   Behaviour 25

Progress 26

Social Support 27

Flexibility 28

Write Down What's Important to You 29

Chapter 3: Motivational Interviewing in Nutrition and Fitness 31

4 Steps of Motivational Interviewing: 32

1. The initial contact: 32

2. Open-caring: 32

3. Active Listening: 33

4. Exhortation and Encouragement: 33

What is Motivational Interviewing in Nutrition and Fitness? 33

The basic principles of motivational interviewing are as follows: 35

Motivational Interviewing: How Does it Work? 35

The following are commonly used motivational interviewing techniques: 39

Chapter 4: Using Motivational Interviewing in Nutrition and Fitness 44

Figure 1: Seven-Stage Wellness Plan 45

Figure 2: Motivational Interviewing Techniques Used Throughout the Seven Stages of a Wellness Plan..................45

Figure 3: From Motivational Interviewing to Client Success 46

    Step One: Motivational Assessment...................47

    Step Two: Goal Clarification 48

Figure 4: Motivational Interviewing Techniques used in Goal Clarification 49

    Step Three: Action Planning....................51

    Step Four: Monitoring and Evaluation 51

    Step Five: Problem Solving 52

    Step Six: Goal Setting and Re-evaluation............53

    Step Seven: Evaluation and Follow-Up 53

Chapter 5: Working with Stages of Change as a Motivational Interviewing Strategy in Nutrition and Fitness 55

    Stage 1: Precontemplation 55

    Stage 2: Contemplation 56

    Stage 3: Preparation................56

    Stage 4: Action........................56

Stage 5: Maintenance 57
Stage 6: Relapse 57
Stage 7: Termination 57

Chapter 6: Other Motivational Interviewing Strategies in Nutrition and Fitness 65

Struggling with nutrition or fitness? Here are a few other interview techniques you can use: 65

The following additional motivational interviewing techniques can be useful in nutrition and fitness: . 66

Chapter 7: Overcoming Barriers to Change 72

Recognizing Resistance to Change 73

The Top 10 Barriers to Change 75

Do You Really Want to Change Your Eating Habits? 79

The 3-Week Diet: Your Lifestyle Transformation Starts Now 80

Chapter 8: Common Issues In Nutrition and Fitness (Part I) - Motivational Interviewing. 83

Common Issues In Nutrition and Fitness (Part II) - The Relationship Of Nutrition And Exercise To Health and Disease 86

Lifestyle Choices & The Effect on Health 89

Here are a few common lifestyle choices that can be improved upon to overall improve your health:.... 90

Common Issues In Nutrition and Fitness (Part 1) - The Role of Diet and Exercise in Health and Disease 93

Chapter 9: New Developments in Nutrition and Fitness 94

Research Findings that Have a Direct Bearing on Nutrition and Fitness 95

Chapter 10: Common Issues In Nutrition and Fitness (Part II) - Motivational Interviewing 104

Chapter 11: Issues With Motivational Interviewing in Nutrition and Fitness 113

A client's motivation can be low for many reasons, including the following: 113

The core beliefs of a client may include any of the following: 117

Here are some questions that can be helpful in motivational interviewing: 119

Conclusion 124

Introduction

Motivational interviewing (MI) has been studied in a variety of settings. In eating disorder counselling, MI may be a useful approach to addressing ambivalence. Although the term "motivational interviewing" was first coined by Miller and Rollnick in 1991, its roots are traced back to the early work of Tice and Baumeister in 1980[1]. According to Bannan-Ritland, it is not enough for counsellor and client to have an agreement on goals if the client lacks the motivation or ability to achieve those goals. Bannan-Ritland proposes that MI can be used to help clients overcome ambivalence by teaching them how to talk about and explore their own motives. It is believed that the "client's sense of their own personal agency will be strengthened, leading them to feel greater responsibility for their actions".

Theoretical Model

Miller and Rollnick describe a cyclical model of change in which ambivalence follows each stage of change. The stages of change include pre-contemplation, contemplation, preparation, action and maintenance. Following each stage are two reactions: resistance and denial. Resistance can be seen as the client's reaction to the suggestion that he/she might benefit from changing. Denial, in the case of dieting and weight loss, occurs when the client is convinced he/she does not need to make a change. Weight-related ambivalence may be caused by a combination of biological and psychological factors. Biological risk factors include insulin resistance, abdominal fat deposition, leptin (a hormone produced by fat cells) levels, central fat deposition and breast-to-waist ratio. Psychological risk factors include low self-esteem, negative body image, dissatisfaction with weight and shape, depression and self-stigma.

In MI, the two reactions are used as an opportunity to help the client overcome ambivalence. Clients may experience a turning point in which the negative feelings related to making changes are replaced with feelings of hope. This is often referred to as "defusion" and involves three steps: make it safe for the client to talk about their values and goals, help them discover their own reasons for change, and teach them how to make changes.

When approaching clients who are ambivalent about making positive lifestyle changes, it is important to be aware of their readiness, or level of motivation for change. Motivation may be influenced by a variety of factors, including physiological factors such as age and gender. Cultural factors include an individual's upbringing, religion and socioeconomic status. People who are members of the working class or lower class are more likely to be heavier because of decreased access to healthier food choices and increased time pressures. Gender may also play a role, with women more likely to diet and weigh themselves than men, possibly because societal images influence women's body image more than men's body image.

Chapter 1: A New Approach to Nutrition and Fitness

Nutrition and fitness are integrative aspects of health, and ones that affect us in every aspect of our lives. We cannot escape them, even temporarily. However, in our consumerist society, we are constantly bombarded with products that claim to "add five pounds to your bench press in one month!" or "burn off those undesirable pounds without dieting!" These claims do not provide the information necessary for us to be responsible consumers who can make informed decisions on these matters. To counter this type of misinformation, it is important that you understand the information behind nutrition and fitness so that you can form your own opinions on the process of staying healthy and how you can appropriately tailor a program to yourself.

Any program you devise can be broken down into three areas: nutrition, fitness and psychological. In this book I will discuss the role of psychology in health and fitness, especially as it relates to "diets." My discussion will centre around motivational interviewing and how it can be used in the field of nutrition and fitness for the purpose of facilitating behavioural change.

Motivational interviewing can only be viewed as a perspective or a framework for understanding nutritional behaviour. Anyone who has been involved with medical nutrition therapy or cognitive/behavioural weight loss programs knows that the failure rate is incredible. The average dieter loses a mere four pounds after one year of participation in a weight loss program, and studies show that the longer you are on a diet, the less likely you are to lose weight. The medical community tends to look at this from the "Eskimo" hypothesis—if you are cold, it is because you have too many calories. If this were true, all native inhabitants of warm weather climates would be overweight! According to Shick and Weintraub (2002), "the fact that all people of high-risk populations, such as those with obesity or diabetes, do not develop these diseases means that obesity has environmental and genetic factors. Dieting to lose weight is one such factor."

The "environment" that contributes to obesity is, of course, the food we eat. Although you can put an obese person on a diet, you cannot put a skinny person on a diet. The difference is in the behaviour of the two people. Skinny people have learned to control their eating; they have learned not to eat as much and when they do eat, their choices are much healthier than those of most obese people. This means that skinny people don't develop obesity-related health problems; they learn what behaviours will lead them towards these conditions (i.e., putting forth little physical effort) and what behaviours will lead them away from these conditions (i.e. working out "just a little harder."). In successful people, the behaviours are internalized and become part of the person. If you put a high risk person on a diet, they will still act like a high risk person. They will still go to places that offer unhealthy foods rather than healthier ones. They will not learn how to alter their behaviour in order to change their health status.

Motivation is also an important factor in changing behaviour, but motivation is not enough. People don't want motivation; they want performance. They want results. Motivational interviewing is a way of helping a person learn how to become self-motivated, rather than having motivation come from outside sources. This becomes important in the fitness field because when you are selling motivation and performance, the person receiving it has a lot more control over the situation.

Motivational Interviewing: What is it?

Motivational interviews are different from many other types of psychological work because they work from the assumption that the individual has an inner drive for healthy behaviours. Motivational interviewing uses this drive to help people overcome obstacles that prevent them from enacting these behaviours. This process also attempts to help clients recognize their own motivations for change and incorporate them into their own behaviour change plan.

The framework upon which this work is based is called the Tran theoretical Model, a continuum that describes the stages of change. The Tran theoretical Model was initially created by Prochaska and DiClemente (1983) as an extension of stage models from the Diagnostic and Statistical Manual of Mental Disorders IV as outlined by Shiffman (1988). They stated, "for any given health behaviour, people differ in their readiness to change." This fundamental understanding of how change takes place has far-reaching implications in both fields.

Chapter 2: Current Status of Nutrition and Fitness

The current state of the world's nutrition and fitness is not only a problem in the United States. Worldwide, obesity and malnutrition are on the rise. In addition, some people in the United States may be at risk for depletion of nutrients because they do not have access to healthy food options or lack knowledge about how to prepare nutritious meals (Gittelsohn & Marks 18).

We know from research that when we don't eat enough fruits and vegetables or drink enough water, we can become malnourished – which can lead to weight gain, poor health, fatigue – even death. We can also get too large a portion size, even though we may think we've eaten a healthy meal. It's also important to remember that what you eat is not as important as the amount of food you eat. Studies have found that people who consume less fat and more fruits and vegetables are healthier than those who consume more saturated fat and less fruits and vegetables (Gittelsohn & Marks 23).

Moreover, it's alarming that many Americans have gained weight over the years – even when they do try to eat healthy. Our access to fast food restaurants makes it easy for us to choose unhealthy foods without thinking about whether we should be eating these foods or not. However, as we become more aware of the negative health consequences associated with eating too much fast food, we may make healthier choices in the future.

The truth is that willpower isn't always enough to help us make healthy nutrition and fitness choices. You may really want to lose weight, but if you find yourself eating ice cream every night after dinner or constantly choosing fast food instead of fruits and vegetables, your willpower isn't working for you. To improve our nutrition and fitness, we need more than just willpower – we need to overcome our ambivalence about making changes in our behaviour.

Ambivalence

One of the most common reasons people don't stick to their nutrition and fitness goals is that they are ambivalent about achieving these goals. On one hand, they want to make healthy changes in their behaviour, but on the other hand, they are afraid of making major changes. We have already established that eating healthy and exercising can be hard. They require a lot of time and effort – especially when we are already tired from a long day at work. We may not be sure that these efforts will pay off in the long run.

If we are ambivalent about making changes to our nutrition and fitness behaviours, we may find it even more difficult to motivate ourselves to eat healthier meals or exercise regularly. If we want to lose weight but aren't 100% sure that it's necessary for us, then we're more likely to give up on our weight loss goals. We may not believe that our weight really is that high, or we might think we don't have the time or energy to think about any major changes in our behaviour.

To prevent ambivalence from getting in the way of your nutrition and fitness goals, you may want to ask yourself these questions:

What makes you want to start eating healthier meals and exercising more often?

How powerful is your need to do these things? Four levels of need include "must," "should," "want" and "no reason." How motivated are you to begin making some changes in your behaviour? To find out where your motivation lies on this spectrum, ask yourself which level of need you feel right now. Are you at a "must" level, a level where you really feel that you must do this? Are you at a "should" level, where your motivation is stronger than it was in the past but not as strong as it could be? Or are you at a "want" level, where your motivation isn't so strong and you probably would not make any changes if someone wasn't pushing you to do it? (Seaman & Seaman; Zuckerman et al. 22).

What are your thoughts about changing your nutrition and fitness behaviours?

For example, if you're thinking that it's too hard to eat healthy and exercise regularly, then you are likely ambivalent about making changes. However, if you are thinking that it's not hard or that you will feel better if you eat healthier meals and exercise more regularly, then the tide may be in your favour. Whether or not you believe these statements may determine whether or not you continue to make changes in your nutrition and fitness behaviours (Seaman & Seaman; Zuckerman et al. 22).

How much do you believe these statements about making changes in your nutrition and fitness behaviours?

If you don't agree with these statements, you may be even more ambivalent about changing your behaviour than before you began reading this book. But if you agree with some or all of these statements, you are probably thinking in a more positive manner about making changes in your behaviour. This is an important step toward reaching your goals (Seaman & Seaman; Zuckerman et al. 22).

Beliefs

If our beliefs about nutrition and fitness weren't powerful enough to influence our thoughts, behaviours and preferences, then they would have no control over what we eat and how active we are every day. In fact, our beliefs have such influence over us that they can even make the food we eat cause us to gain weight. Because of this power, it's important to explore your beliefs about nutrition and fitness.

If you believe that nothing works for weight loss, then it will be nearly impossible to lose weight. If you believe that you are genetically predisposed to gaining weight, it may be harder to stop your eating and exercise habits. If you believe that it's just too hard or too time consuming to make changes in your nutrition and fitness behaviours, then it may be tough for you to make changes.

Beliefs can help us gain strength as well as hinder us from reaching our goals. For example, if a belief such as "I will never lose weight" exists in our minds, then we might stop trying entirely in order to avoid failure. Equally harmful is the belief that "It's impossible for me to lose weight so I'll just give up." This type of belief can cause you to stop thinking about making changes altogether. Either way, it can be difficult to reach your nutrition and fitness goals when these beliefs exist in your mind (Seaman & Seaman; Zuckerman et al. 23).

Do you have any beliefs that may be holding you back or preventing you from making changes? If so, consider if changing any of these negative beliefs into more positive ones will help you reach your goals (Seaman & Seaman; Zuckerman et al. 23).

Motivation

Just as the belief that nothing works for weight loss can hinder you from reaching your goals, the belief that nothing works may actually be motivating to you. If you think that nothing works, then maybe there is no point in trying to lose weight. If you believe that it's completely hopeless and won't work for you, then perhaps you won't waste time trying. The truth is, such beliefs may indeed work to your advantage when it comes to making changes. But remember: It will cause problems later on if this belief prevents you from taking action toward your goals (Seaman & Seaman; Zuckerman et al. 24).

If you have this belief, you need to consider why it motivated you to take action. What was the motivating factor, and can it help you reach your goals? Was it a fear of getting older and becoming overweight? Was it a desire for a new, slimmer image? Did someone say something that caused this motivation to occur? Can you determine what caused that motivation so that when motivation strikes again, you can take action toward meeting your goals? Then the next time around, find ways of motivating yourself besides telling yourself nothing works. Believe in your ability to make changes and in your ability to succeed with these changes (Seaman & Seaman; Zuckerman et al. 24). Another thing you might want to consider is to find an outside source of motivation, such as a support group. Not only will a support group help you feel better about yourself, but it can keep you on track with your goals. Having people to talk to about your troubles will make the process less frustrating, and it might even help your friends motivate you further (Seaman & Seaman). The next time you feel like nothing is working and that the dieting or exercise program you are on isn't working either, think back on the success stories in this research project and use those stories to keep yourself inspired.

Behaviour

The way you do anything is the way you do everything. Whether you are trying to lose weight, learn a new language, or quit smoking, if your nutrition and fitness behaviours are not strong then it's unlikely that those efforts will pay off in the long term. For example, if we want to lose weight but we don't eat healthy or exercise regularly, then we may give up when we see that our efforts aren't working. And if we are eating healthy but don't exercise regularly, then perhaps that is why we aren't losing weight as fast as we would like. In both of these situations, our efforts may be more successful if our behaviour is more balanced. In fact, the best nutrition and fitness behaviours we can have centre on eating healthy meals, exercising regularly, getting enough sleep and making progress toward our goals (Seaman & Seaman; Zuckerman et al. 30).

To be successful at changing our nutrition and fitness behaviours, we need to know what the best behaviour patterns are for success. By examining the research and looking at the examples in this book, you should be able to determine what works for you and what doesn't work so that your behaviours are balanced enough to keep you on track with your goals (Seaman & Seaman; Zuckerman et al. 30). The following are some common behaviours that might help you reach your goals.

Progress

One behaviour that is often associated with success is progress. When we make progress toward reaching our goals, we are more likely to continue trying to reach them. This in itself can be a powerful motivator for many people, and it's important for us to consider, whether our goal is weight loss, getting in shape or learning something new (Seaman & Seaman; Zuckerman et al. 31).

To ensure that you are making progress toward your goals, set realistic expectations for yourself. It may be hard to lose 15 pounds in a month, but if that was your goal, it would not be realistic and might create a negative attitude about losing weight. By setting realistic expectations, you can better understand how to achieve your goals in small steps – and these small steps will result in big strides over time (Seaman & Seaman; Zuckerman et al. 31).

Social Support

As we learned earlier in the chapter, support from other people can make our goals seem more achievable and can help us stay on track with meeting those goals. Therefore, it is important to remember that social support can be an effective behaviour for changing our nutrition and fitness behaviours. If you have family or friends who are supporting you in your efforts to lose weight or get into shape, then use them as a resource.

For example, if you are trying to lose weight and you are having a tough time with it, consider talking with your friend or family member about your progress so far. Ask how they have been able to do this before and why they are having success now. If they have had trouble losing weight or getting in shape, then use what they tell you to help motivate you. By talking about your goals with others, you can make it more likely that you will achieve them (Seaman & Seaman; Zuckerman et al. 31).

Flexibility

When we are trying to reach our goals, there are going to be days when we want to give up. But if we wait until that time comes, then we might just lose the chance to succeed and meet our goals. Therefore, it's important to have strategies for reaching your goals in ways that can help you succeed when the going gets tough.

For example, if you are trying to lose weight and you find yourself struggling on a day when you really wanted to reach your goal, then consider skipping dessert that night. If you had a difficult time working out at the gym, do an exercise video at home or go for a brisk walk around your neighbourhood. Consider changing your nutrition and fitness behaviours so that they suit your body and lifestyle better (Seaman & Seaman; Zuckerman et al. 31).

When you do this, your goals can still be met even though you may not have met them exactly as you had originally planned. Another way to be flexible with your goals is to develop a "Plan B" when reaching those goals is impossible and would not be in your best interest. For example, if you are trying to lose weight but don't want to skip dessert every night, then consider eating a small dessert just once each week (Seaman & Seaman; Zuckerman et al. 31).

Write Down What's Important to You

Many of the participants in this research project found that writing down their goals was an important strategy for reaching them. For example, if you are trying to lose weight, writing down your goals can make them more concrete and can make it easier to go back to them when you need guidance. As one participant said, "Writing it down keeps me on track."

If you don't write your goals down and just keep them in your mind, they are a lot more likely to be forgotten. This is because it will be harder to remember what your goals are when they occur randomly throughout the day (Seaman & Seaman; Zuckerman et al. 32). Therefore, make sure that you write down your goals and use them to guide your nutrition and fitness behaviours all day long. Maybe also take this advice from one of the participants: "I keep the list in my purse, and it's always with me."

The next time you want to reach a goal or improve your nutrition or fitness behaviours, write down what is important to you for meeting those goals. This will not only help you remember why you want to reach those goals but will also help you learn what works for reaching them (Seaman & Seaman; Zuckerman et al. 32).

Chapter 3: Motivational Interviewing in Nutrition and Fitness

Motivational interviewing is an evidence-based technique designed to help clients overcome ambivalence, break free from diets and overcome barriers to change. It is a form of counselling that seeks to empower individuals by helping them understand their own concerns, perceptions and feelings about the behaviour change process (e.g., dieting) so they can make more informed decisions that are right for them.

The research studied and demonstrated the efficacy of motivational interviewing in four main settings: college students exploring healthy eating alternatives, addictive behaviours such as smoking cessation or cutting back on alcohol consumption, chronic disease management, and exercise participation among adolescent girls with low levels of physical activity.

When trying to help clients make permanent change, it has been shown that the most effective way is to help them work through the process of change collaboratively. It is important to help them understand their ambivalence and fears about making a change. This understanding allows for clients to feel comfortable with the process of making a change and once they feel more confident, they are more likely to implement changes effectively.

4 Steps of Motivational Interviewing:

1. The initial contact: This process begins with assessing the client's readiness for change. One must assess what stage of readiness clients are in before implementing a plan of action. This assessment is based on a client's personal motivation and desire for change.

2. Open-caring: The counsellor must convey a caring attitude toward the client while also being

honest and direct about the negative consequences of their behaviour (based on previous research).

3. Active Listening: The counsellor must be an active listening partner to the client and assist them in identifying discrepancies between what they desire for themselves and their current behaviour (healthy eating, exercise, etc.).

4. Exhortation and Encouragement: The counsellor must offer positive reinforcement to the clients for intrinsic behaviour change.

What is Motivational Interviewing in Nutrition and Fitness?

Motivational interviewing provides a framework for helping clients make behaviour change by helping them address their ambivalence, fears and perceived barriers to change. It also helps the client accept personal responsibility for making changes and involves offering positive encouragement during the change process. This counselling approach is utilized with many different populations facing various behavioural health challenges including nutrition/fitness, smoking cessation or reduced alcohol consumption. Motivational interviewing can be utilized with individuals who are looking to improve eating habits, exercise more often, lose weight, etc.

Motivational interviewing is a brief, directive style of communication that is most effective when used in a one-on-one setting between counsellor and client. The counsellor works collaboratively with the client to build rapport, while also providing support and positive encouragement throughout the process. Motivational interviewing utilizes four steps to help clients move through an informed decision-making process that includes exploration of ambivalence, barriers and discrepancies which can assist in working toward permanent change in behaviour (i.e., nutrition/fitness).

The basic principles of motivational interviewing are as follows:

Motivational Interviewing: How Does it Work?

There is a growing body of research that demonstrates that motivational interviewing is effective for helping clients make behaviour change in a variety of health behaviours. It has been used successfully with nicotine addiction, weight loss, exercise adherence and dietary change. Motivational interviewing is based on the idea that some people are more motivated to change than others. It assumes that people have the capacity to take responsibility for their behaviour and make positive changes even in the presence of external pressures or obstacles (i.e., diet, exercise). It is a collaborative approach between the counsellor and client that is directive in nature. The counsellor helps the client make change by focusing on their concerns/fears/feelings, addressing ambivalence to change, supporting intrinsic motivation for behaviour change, providing encouragement during the process and reinforcing positive behaviours. Through this process, clients gain confidence in their ability to handle challenges they face in making positive lifestyle changes. Motivational interviewing aims to empower clients with the skills they need to address barriers and strengthen personal motivations toward making behaviour changes that are healthy and beneficial for them.

In five studies conducted with college students who were exploring healthy eating alternatives, motivational interviewing techniques made a significant difference in students' ability to develop healthy eating habits. Students who underwent motivational interviewing reported more positive eating behaviours and a decreased desire for sweet foods than those in the control group. Power and colleagues found that motivational interviewing was effective with college students interested in quitting smoking. These students reported higher levels of motivation to abstain from smoking after receiving motivational interviewing and demonstrated increased levels of abstinence several months afterward.

Motivational interviewing is also effective in helping clients overcome ambivalence about exercise by identifying barriers that may prevent them from participating in physical activity. It has been shown to be successful with adolescent girls who have low levels of physical activity as well as those who are at high risk for developing type 2 diabetes. Motivational interviewing has also been shown to be effective at helping clients who are trying to reduce the amount of alcohol they consume. When combined with problem-solving skills, motivational interviewing with heavy drinkers led to significant positive change in drinking habits.

Motivational interviewing has also been studied for use as a weight loss intervention for obese and overweight adults. In this study, participants were randomly assigned to either receive motivational interviewing or a control condition. Both groups received information about healthy eating and physical activity, but the motivational interviewing group was encouraged to explore psychological factors that may deter them from making lifestyle changes. This group had more positive outcomes than the control group. They lost more weight and had a greater decrease in BMI.

Motivational interviewing is useful in reducing the effects of stress, anger and hostility among individuals with chronic diseases, such as depression, diabetes, and cancer. Additionally, motivational interviewing has been found to be effective for increasing adherence to medications by people with HIV/AIDS.

A study conducted by Luzard & Mitchell (2001) found that motivational interviewing is an appropriate counselling method for promoting health at all ages from school-aged children to older adults. Although this study is not presented for the purpose of convincing individuals to adopt health behaviours, it does provide empirical support that motivational interviewing techniques are effective.

It has been widely believed that and recovering alcoholics and addicts should avoid people, places, or events that could stir up cravings for alcohol. However, a 2007 study by O'Brien &

Hester found that this technique was not as effective as motivational interviewing when comparing the two methods. It is suggested that motivational interviewing techniques should be considered as a method for relapse prevention after detoxification from alcoholism or drug addiction.

Motivational interviewing has been used in treatment programs to help people overcome addictions.

The following are commonly used motivational interviewing techniques:

This technique is used when the client has an active problem. The counsellor will ask the client to describe the situation, empathize, and then help to clarify the consequences of continuing with that behaviour. In more complex situations, the counsellor will discuss each consequence with the client and ask how they feel about that consequence. By sharing how they feel about a specific consequence, it can allow them to experience cognitive dissonance which is having two conflicting ideas at one time. That in turn will then motivate them to want to change their behaviour.

Lack of motivation can be attributed to many factors such as poor social support or negative feelings about treatment or recovery itself. Motivational Interviewing helps people to find their own reasons for change instead of relying solely on external sources.

This technique is used when the client has an historical addiction or fails to do something planned. The counsellor will ask questions about what was learned that will help the client understand why they made the mistake and what they could have done differently. The counsellor then works to get the client to form a plan that is more likely to be successful, and clients are encouraged with positive feedback.

Habits can be described as behaviours that are repeated over and over again through routine. Routines can be both helpful or harmful. This technique focuses on trying to create new habits for good behaviours rather than eliminating bad ones. The goal is to create an environment that makes it easy to do the desired behaviour.

As addiction progresses, it becomes less about the pleasurable effects of a substance and more about managing the pain caused by its absence. The maintenance stage focuses on helping clients improve their ability to cope with life's stresses and maintain abstinence for longer periods of time. This stage helps clients build a solid foundation for long-term recovery while focusing on learning new skills through continued counselling support.

Motivational Interviewing is a counselling technique that allows the client control over their treatment and recovery process instead of letting it be controlled by others. This process empowers the client to reach their own recovery goals.

Methadone Maintenance is unique because it utilizes medication to reduce or eliminate symptoms of withdrawal and physical cravings. It can be very effective in helping individuals overcome addiction and create a solid foundation for long-term recovery while focusing on learning new skills through continued counselling support.

Naltrexone is an opioid receptor antagonist that helps prevent the effects of opiates on the body's receptors. Naltrexone is typically used after detoxification to help individuals maintain recovery and avoid relapse.

Narcotics Anonymous is a 12-step program designed for those with addictive behaviours involving opiate drugs such as heroin, morphine, and opium. Members meet regularly to discuss their struggles with addiction.

The Twelve Steps are guidelines for individuals in NA trying to maintain abstinence from drugs and alcohol. The Twelve Traditions are guidelines that help NA groups function more smoothly and efficiently.

SMART Recovery is a self-empowering program designed for those experiencing addictive behaviours related to drugs and alcohol or other life issues such as eating disorders, sex addiction, gambling addiction or any other unmanageable problem. Members meet regularly to discuss their struggles with these issues using the SMART Recovery tools which include: building motivation, managing urges, abstaining from substances, positive lifestyle changes and relapse prevention.

Chapter 4: Using Motivational Interviewing in Nutrition and Fitness

In the previous chapter we explored how counsellors can use motivational interviewing in nutrition and fitness counselling to help clients overcome ambivalence, break free from diets, and overcome barriers to change. In this chapter we will review how utilizing motivational interviewing techniques throughout the seven stages of a wellness plan can be used to increase client success.

Figure 1: Seven-Stage Wellness Plan

Counsellors utilizing motivational interviewing techniques through the seven stages of a wellness plan can increase client motivation and engagement in the process. In doing so, counsellors can lead clients to the best possible outcomes. In this chapter, we will explore how motivational interviewing techniques that are used in step one (motivational assessment) and step seven (reflective consultation) may be used throughout the seven stages of a wellness plan.

Figure 2: Motivational Interviewing Techniques Used Throughout the Seven Stages of a Wellness Plan

Clients who come to counsellors to discuss setting wellness goals may or may not be motivated to make changes. These clients will benefit from motivational interviewing techniques that can be used at all seven steps of the wellness plan. Other clients may already be motivated but appreciate the input, and suggestions, of their counsellor. In this case, the client is still likely to benefit from motivational interviewing techniques especially in steps two (goal clarification), three (planning), five (action steps), and six (maintenance).

Figure 3: From Motivational Interviewing to Client Success

The stages of the seven-stage wellness plan are designed to increase client motivation and engagement in the process, but they also contribute to client success. The cycle at the bottom of figure 3 is a simplified representation of how motivational interviewing techniques contribute to client success.

In steps one and two (motivational assessment and goal clarification) counsellors use motivational interviewing techniques such as open-ended questions and reflective listening to help clients become motivated about setting goals. In step three (planning) counsellors use motivational interviewing techniques such as reflection, prompting, empathy, summarizing, and norm-setting to help clients set specific goals that can be achieved in 5-7 days. In steps five and seven (action steps and reflective consultation) counsellors use motivational interviewing techniques such as asking questions, offering solutions, summarizing, empathy, and positive reframing to help clients plan their action steps toward reaching those goals. In step six (maintenance) counsellors use motivational interviewing techniques like positive reframing and empathy to help maintain client success once they have reached their wellness goals. By utilizing motivational interviewing techniques throughout the seven-step wellness plan counsellors can guide clients to the best possible outcomes.

In this chapter we will review how motivational interviewing techniques can be used in each of the seven stages of a wellness plan.

Step One: Motivational Assessment

In step one (motivational assessment) counsellors use motivational interviewing techniques to determine if the client is motivated to make behaviour change, and if not, what level of motivation the client has. Using open-ended questions such as "What are your reasons for coming today?" and "What are your hopes for our meeting?" counsellors can uncover what is motivating the client. If a client does not come in with any real motivation for making a change then counsellors must first elicit that motivation. When we elicit this motivation we are able to uncover why our clients want to make changes. This allows us to address their ambivalence and motivate them toward action. If our clients enter our offices with motivation to make changes, then counsellors can use motivational interviewing techniques to help them clarify and refine that motivation toward action.

Step Two: Goal Clarification

In step two (goal clarification) counsellors use motivational interviewing techniques to uncover a client's past goals and future goals regarding their behaviour change. Using open-ended questions such as "What is your hope for your future?" and "What was your experience with setting goals before coming into counselling?" counsellors are able to learn about what kind of goals will motivate their clients. If a client has not set any goals then counsellors must first help them clarify what they want for their future. After the client has clarified what they want in the future, then counsellors can help them clarify how they will achieve those goals.

Figure 4: Motivational Interviewing Techniques used in Goal Clarification

Counsellors must use motivational interviewing techniques throughout goal clarification. For instance, if a client says that they want to begin an exercise program but that they do not know where to begin, then counsellors can employ reflective listening statements such as "I hear you saying that you don't know where to begin with starting an exercise program . Is that right?" By repeating what the client has said in a way that is not leading counsellors can help clients clarify what is getting in the way of them setting their goals. After reflecting back to clients, counsellors can use reflective questions such as "What do you think would help you begin an exercise program?" and "What are some things that would be hard for you to begin an exercise program?". These questions encourage the client to think about how they have reached goals in the past and how they can apply those methods moving forward.

Counsellors must use motivational interviewing techniques throughout goal clarification. With each goal that is clarified counsellors must drill down into every sub goal. For instance, if a client wants to exercise three times a week for 30 minutes then counsellors would want to know why they want to exercise three times a week for 30 minutes. Counsellors could ask "What is your hope for exercising three times a week?" and "How do you dream of exercising three times a week?". Counsellors could also ask about different reasons why the client wants to exercise three times a week. For instance, level one reasons might include "I want better health" and level two reasons might include "I want more energy". After asking about different reasons that motivate the client to exercise three times a week, counsellors could next ask about the different obstacles that are getting in the way of this client exercising three times a week. For instance, level one obstacles might include "I don't think that I have time" and level two obstacles might include "I feel tired by the end of my workday". By drilling down into all these sub goals counsellors can help clients clarify their goals and figure out what they need to do to achieve their goals.

Step Three: Action Planning

In step three (action planning) counsellors use motivational interviewing techniques to help clients determine what they will need to do to achieve their goals. For instance, if a client wants to lose weight counsellors could ask "What would you like to do or not do to lose weight?". Then, the client could explain that they want to track what they eat and get in shape. Next, counsellors could ask "Is there anything else that you want to track?" or "What would be difficult for you about tracking what you eat?". The client might say that they do not like writing things down or keeping a food journal. Then counsellors can help the client brainstorm different ways that they can keep track of their calories.

Step Four: Monitoring and Evaluation

In step four (monitoring and evaluation) counsellors will monitor and evaluate their clients' progress throughout goal achievement. This can be done in a number of ways. For instance, counsellors could have the client keep track of their progress on a daily basis and then they could go over the client's progress at their next session. Another option is for the counsellor to give the clients self-monitoring forms that they can either keep in their phones or write down on paper and bring back to their next appointment.

Step Five: Problem Solving

In step five (problem solving) counsellors will help clients problem solve any obstacles that they have encountered when trying to achieve their goals. The goal is for the counsellor to help the client see all obstacles as challenges rather than threats.

It is also important that counsellors do not offer too much advice or solutions to their client's problems. For example, if the client is having difficulty sticking to a certain diet while weight loss counselling, it may be best for the counsellor to ask what attempts they have already made to solve this problem and how those attempts have been unsuccessful.

Step Six: Goal Setting and Re-evaluation

In step six (goal setting and re-evaluation), counsellors will help clients evaluate their goals and identify new goals that they may want to work towards. It is very common for clients to change their minds about what they want or need throughout goal achievement. Therefore, it is important for counsellors to help the client determine whether the goals that they set are realistic and attainable. It is also very important for counsellors to make sure that the client has a plan on how they will achieve their goal.

Step Seven: Evaluation and Follow-Up

The last step in problem solving counselling is evaluation and follow-up. In this step, counsellors will evaluate whether or not the client has completed their plan as well as assess if there are any problems that have been left unsolved. Depending on what needs to be done, counsellors may or may not "follow up" with clients to make sure they are completing their plans and goals successfully.

Motivational interviewing techniques are a useful tool in nutrition and fitness counselling because they reduce resistance and increase client motivation to follow through with stage-appropriate action plans. The seven-stage wellness plan was designed to gradually bring clients along the readiness continuum from avoidance to action. Motivational interviewing techniques help clients move along this continuum by reducing ambivalence, breaking clients free from disordered eating patterns, improving client self-efficacy, and helping clients manage barriers to change. Counsellors can utilize motivational interviewing techniques at each stage of the wellness plan as well as throughout the process of achieving goals. Using motivational interviewing techniques in this way can guide clients toward successful outcomes.

Chapter 5: Working with Stages of Change as a Motivational Interviewing Strategy in Nutrition and Fitness

Stage 1: Precontemplation

This stage includes those who have not yet made the decision to make a change. In this stage, individuals make excuses to avoid making changes and may even be convinced that they are unable to change their behaviour. The key here is to help them understand the benefits of changing and show them how manageable it really is.

Stage 2: Contemplation

This stage includes those who have become aware of an issue and are considering making changes in their lifestyle, but have not yet done so. We focus on discussing the pros or cons of making a lifestyle change from both perspectives, so that they can see which option best suits them.

Stage 3: Preparation

This stage includes those who have decided to change their lifestyle and are trying to figure out how. We focus on figuring out the best plan of action for the individual, taking into account their current lifestyle and stress. We also address any underlying habits that might be contributing to the behaviour. For example, if someone is eating out more often because they are bored or lonely, we might want to focus on appropriate ways they can entertain themselves or find companionship.

Stage 4: Action

This stage includes those who have successfully changed their behaviour or made strides in doing so. We then move on to discussing healthy ways of maintaining this change, and what types of things that might jeopardize it.

Stage 5: Maintenance

This stage includes those who have successfully changed their behaviour or made strides in doing so. We then move on to discussing healthy ways of maintaining this change, and what types of things that might jeopardize it. This group also includes those who have mastered changes and are able to maintain them indefinitely.

Stage 6: Relapse

We discuss relapse scenarios so that clients understand what may lead to a relapse and how they might avoid doing so. Most relapses happen within the first 3 months; therefore it is important to focus on planning for relapse prevention early in the process.

Stage 7: Termination

This stage includes those who have successfully changed their behaviour or made strides in doing so. We then move on to discussing healthy ways of maintaining this change, and what types of things that might jeopardize it. This group also includes those who have mastered changes and are able to maintain them indefinitely.

Unlike other methods, MI uses an interview technique that is not cantered on the delivery of information, but rather on communicating understanding and empathy. Instead of telling a client how to change their behaviour, the counsellor asks questions that help the client explore their own thoughts and feelings about their belief system. This method allows the counsellor to help the client determine what motivates them, which leads to a change in behaviour. When using MI for weight loss, counsellors should focus on helping clients move forward and control their eating so that they can maintain a healthy weight loss and not gain back any weight. A study conducted in Hong Kong tested the effectiveness of MI compared to a control group on helping obese children lose weight and maintain an ideal weight after treatment. The intervention was effective at helping children lose weight initially but did not help with long-term maintenance of an ideal body mass index (BMI). However, BMI scores were able to predict the likelihood of a child maintaining his or her ideal weight. This study shows that counselling is effective in helping participants lose weight but not in helping them maintain their ideal weight. Another study found that adults who received MI counselling lost more weight initially then those who did not receive the same counselling, however they did not maintain their weight loss for a long period of time - within the first 12 weeks over half of the people in each group had gained back their initial pounds.

A great deal of research has been done on MI and its use as an intervention for nutrition and fitness clients. It has been proven one of the most effective methods for helping clients in general. The majority of research done on MI has been in the area of weight management. While many studies do show its effectiveness as an intervention method for weight loss, no research has been done to show whether or not healthy people can benefit from MI. Many researchers suggest that this counselling method would be ineffective for all but the most ambivalent clients, meaning that those who are undecided about changing their behaviour would benefit from its use. One study showed that those who were more ambivalent and therefore more likely to need motivational interviewing techniques actually responded better to a non-MI group support intervention than an MI intervention group support.

The health professional must also have an understanding of the client's own motivations for wanting to lose weight. If the individual does not truly wish to change his or her lifestyle or behaviour, then motivational interviewing will be ineffective. The counsellor should also be aware of their own motivations for helping the client. It might help to keep in mind that a large portion of most people's problems with weight and diet stem from psychological factors like stress, anxiety, depression, addictions and low self-esteem and confidence rather than from over-eating or lack of fitness. Because these factors can motivate a person to eat more than they should or avoid physical activity, it is important for counsellors to understand what motivates people in general as well as within each specific case.

Though motivational interviewing is often known as a collaborative and non-directive method, the counsellor must still have good boundaries with the client. It is important for the counsellor to remain supportive during the course of therapy, however if they are ineffective in helping their client reach their goals they must be able to let go. They may have to discuss with their client what they would like to do if their goals cannot be met and how they might benefit from ending therapy. The counsellor should also maintain professional boundaries by discussing any outside factors that might motivate a patient's behaviour change such as drug abuse or relationship problems.

In MI the counsellor helps the client identify their internal motivations for change. Self-efficacy (defined as an individual's belief in their ability to succeed at a task) is one of the primary motivations that clients need to possess in order to be successful in changing their behaviour. The counsellor can help clients understand what they can do and how they might achieve this success.

In addition, it is important for counsellors to help all of their clients create a list of reasons that are unique for each individual which goes along with why it is important to them personally that they lose weight. This list should include both short term and long term benefits of achieving weight loss such as feeling healthier, looking better or regaining physical movement.

Client participation is important in MI. The counsellor aims to assist the client in creating a strategy for change, but it will be their plan and the counsellor does not make decisions for them. This should include all of their life activities, such as diet, exercise and lifestyles. The counsellor helps them to understand how changes they make might affect their lives in positive ways but it is up to the client to put these interventions into place. It is also important for clients to have an understanding of what they can do if they slip up or go off track.

The self-re-evaluation stage is when the client begins to actively change their behaviour and embraces a healthier lifestyle. In order to reinforce this change, the counsellor encourages the client to monitor their progress. This can be achieved by assigning the client a number of tasks such as weighing themselves each week, keeping food journals and record how much exercise they have done that week. Regular contact between the client and counsellor is necessary to keep them accountable.

In the maintenance stage, clients continue leading healthier lifestyles while simultaneously learning what their new lifestyle will include. This stage usually lasts 3 years and involves understanding what issues might arise in their lives when they are not following their plan will help them to determine how they will cope with some of these barriers for future problems. For example, if a client has not been eating a healthy diet and has gained weight, they may be more motivated to stick to their plan if they know that they will be able to recognize when things take a wrong turn and know what steps to take in order to get back on track quickly.

A final stage of the model is termination. This occurs when counsellors believe that clients no longer need their services due to the fact that they are maintaining the new lifestyle and have made sustainable changes. The counsellor should also check with clients on their thoughts about terminating their services with them. This will help the client understand if they have truly changed or if there is more work yet to be done.

Chapter 6: Other Motivational Interviewing Strategies in Nutrition and Fitness

Motivational interviewing can be used in many different situations with clients for diet and fitness. This chapter will present several other motivational interviewing strategies that may prove useful to the practitioner experiencing difficulty or who wants to increase their repertoire of motivational interviewing skills.

Struggling with nutrition or fitness? Here are a few other interview techniques you can use:

"Make no small plans" – Tell your client that in-the-moment success may not translate into long-term results because they're limited by their ambivalence about what they really want.

"What's important?" – Motivational interviewing is fundamentally about helping people figure out what's important to them and then helping them work out how to get it.

"A good place to start" – Help clients clarify their goals, then turn next steps into experiments. Guide clients toward the best method and timing by identifying obstacles (they may not agree with all of these).

The following additional motivational interviewing techniques can be useful in nutrition and fitness:

(1) Ask about the client's thoughts about going back to school for a degree or certification. Then ask if they have considered going back part-time or full-time. If they are not sure whether they would be able to go back, ask them what they are most concerned about. Guide them to the idea that it is OK to inquire about this with their current employer, and suggest that they take the

time to talk to their employer about this. This will help them stay motivated.

(2) Of the people who have gone back for additional education, ask the client how many of these people returned or went back to a job comparable to what they were doing before going back.

(3) Ask the client if they have ever had a plan before and, if so, ask them how that worked for them. If they say it didn't work, ask them what could have been done differently to make it work. This line of questioning may help them develop a plan going forward.

(4) Of course this depends on the client's relationship with their employer and whether or not their employer is open to it. Ask the client if they know anyone who has gone back to school part-time or full-time and how this person was able to arrange their hours or schedule around school. If they are not sure, help them think of someone who works a similar type of job to their own who may have gone back to school. Even if this person is not in the same field as your client,

this will still be helpful for him or her in thinking about how they could arrange their schedule around school.

(5) Find out what the client thinks it would take for them to go back to school part-time or full-time. This can be done by asking, "What do you think it would take?" You can also start by asking the client if they ever thought about going back to school. If they say yes, ask them why they didn't go back. Then, ask if they have ever thought about going back to school. If they say yes, then ask them what would make it easy for them to do this. This will help start the communication process so that you can work with your client on how to achieve their goals through going back to school and sticking with their nutrition and fitness goals.

(6) You can also use motivational interviewing techniques while working out with your client. Use these techniques to help your client stay motivated and on track with their nutrition and fitness goals.

(7) One motivational interviewing technique is to ask the client about their "spirits." Ask them what makes them feel good or bad. Also, ask how often they exercise or work out, how they feel when they do exercise, and if they have any reasons why it seems more difficult for them to stick to working out than it did in the past. If the client says that it always seems more difficult now (and you or someone else did not change anything), this could signal that the client is struggling with stress. This may be due to dieting or working out too hard. Work with them to figure out what, if anything, has changed.

(8) Ask the client if they have been exercising less or not at all. If they say that they have been exercising less than usual, ask them what has been different for them. If the client says that they started a new medication, ask if it makes it difficult for them to exercise more than usual. To help with motivation when starting a new medication, ask the client if there is anything else they could do instead of taking the medication (i.e., other treatments) or take a smaller dose of

the medication so that they don't feel as sick when working out.

(9) If the client says that they have been working out more but eating the same amount of food, you can ask them if they are taking in additional carbohydrates during the day, such as eating whole wheat bread or pasta. If so, then this may prevent them from feeling tired or groggy when working out.

(10) Find out what motivates your client to exercise. You can ask them what they like to do for exercise and if there is anything else they would like to try. Listening to your client's responses can help you gain insight into their motivational level. You can also ask them what their exercise routine looks like and if there is anything that they would like to change about it.

If your client does the research and reads about how many of the diseases we are told to live with are caused by sugar, excessive amounts of carbohydrates in general, and eating gluten products (from wheat, barley, rye and oats) that are not needed in our diet, he or she may be more amenable to switching to a low crab way of eating. I find most people will do what they want to do anyway. The truth will usually come out one way or another when they realize what foods really work for them and what foods cause their body problems. But it was much easier for me to do research and read labels before going to the low crab diet.

Chapter 7: Overcoming Barriers to Change

We know what it's like. You've tried and failed at diet after diet. You've made so many promises to yourself and others that you just can't seem to keep them. There will always be a reason why you should quit, but you have to understand that the reasons for quitting are the ones getting in your way!

We firmly believe in the power of motivational interviewing techniques, a proven interviewing approach pioneered by Dr. William R Miller and Dr. Stephen Rollick who believe that people do want change, but must be "led" rather than "pushed". This book is not about the "five secret steps to weight loss success" (There aren't five and if you know what they are, keep them to yourself.) but rather about the innovative use of motivational interviewing to help people find sustainable solutions to their weight problems.

Motivational interviewing assumes that successful change comes from within. The underlying principle of MI is that change is not motivated by information alone, but also by a person's true need. Thus, the most important element in the change process is helping people identify their own personal reasons for wanting to make a change. Helping them see their barriers will give them the "space" they need to find their own motivation.

Recognizing Resistance to Change

The most important principle of MI is that change happens in steps. You can't move forward until the person "owns" the problem and decides to make a change. This is where motivational interviewing differs from other forms of psychotherapy because it recognizes that people will only take action when they are ready to, not when you want them to or when you think they should. People cannot make changes if they have no desire for them. Yet most health care professionals try to push or coerce their clients into change rather than find out if they really want it.

Resistance to change is a normal reaction. Most people will put off change because it makes them feel uncomfortable. They may have conflicting feelings about the idea of change or they may be so used to being stuck that they don't know where to start. In the next chapter, we'll cover how to help your clients identify their barriers and get past them.

The person who showed up one day for our seminar, "Stress-Free Eating" was a good example of someone who was ready for a change in her weight loss approach and terrified of it at the same time."What if I try this and it doesn't work?" she asked us. "I'll be so disappointed!" we replied. "Disappointed that you are still fat?" Her face said, "Yes, yes I will be." We won her over by letting her know that we thought she could do it—that she was going to be fine even if it didn't work out the way she hoped.

You might assume from this conversation that we are saying all you need to do is remove the barriers to change and your clients will miraculously lose weight. Although this is sometimes true, it's not necessarily going to happen. The issue of weight and health is complicated. Sometimes people need more than a little motivation to shake things up and change their habits. But believing that they can do it, regardless of the outcome, will go a long way toward helping your clients overcome their barriers.

The Top 10 Barriers to Change

In our experience, we've encountered the following ten common barriers to change with our clients:

1. Lack of motivation

2. Listening to negative self-talk

3. Unhealthy role models

4. Lack of positive reinforcement

5. Stress and emotional eating/comfort eating

6. Poor communication with the family/partner/friends about eating habits and body image issues

7. Lack of social support for healthy eating and exercise habits

8. Lack of role models or healthy role models present in the media or popular culture

9. Inaccessible food choices

10. Cultural influences—the social pressures we all feel to fit in

We've also noticed that our clients who have successfully lost weight once or twice often hit speed bumps after a period of time. The good habits they began to develop when they first decided to make a change in their lives start to decline as work and home life become busy and stress increases. We know when we are feeling stressed, it is the last thing we want to think about—exercising, eating right, losing weight. Our motivation takes a hit when the demands on our time increase and yet we still have to find the time or make the space for us. As it turns out, motivation and energy are both "energy-in-motion," requiring action in order for you to keep them. So the challenge is to make healthy lifestyle changes that are so easy and enjoyable that you'll renew your motivation for them often.

Does any of this sound familiar? If you are feeling a little discouraged, it's time to stop thinking about what you think should happen and start thinking about what will happen. Your goals don't have to be big or bold. It is important that whatever they are, they become your goals—not those of someone else who may want you to lose weight because they think it is an inconvenience or a burden. We are going to help you learn how to direct your thoughts toward positive outcomes rather than negative ones and how to follow through with these thoughts in action.

You may have a couple of questions at this point. First, if you were to ask us the one biggest barrier keeping you from losing weight, we would have to tell you that it's not what you think. Many people believe their eating habits are the problem, but in reality they simply haven't developed a fully healthy lifestyle yet that will support their weight loss efforts. That is why it's important to address your motivation for losing weight, as well as all other areas of your life that need improvement so that you can make permanent changes.

Second, if you are worried that you're eating habits are bad and always have been, don't despair. In this book, we will teach you how to change your eating habits and what to do if you slip up. We will share with you strategies to stay on track and how to get back on track after a relapse. The most important thing is for you to realize that taking the steps and actions necessary for change is setting the stage for success.

So what kind of changes are we talking about? The first thing we'd like you to do is think about your energy level and attitude in general. Do you feel awake and energized or tired and lethargic? How would you rate your current eating habits in terms of quality and quantity? Are you eating enough fresh fruits, vegetables, whole grains, lean proteins, and healthy fats? Would you be comfortable telling us about the last time you ate a truly healthy meal or snack daily for one week straight?

Now think about your level of motivation to lose weight. Are you ready to take the next step and take action? Do you have a specific goal in mind? If so, we applaud your commitment. If not, that's okay too. Keep reading and follow the recommendations we make specifically for you. Regardless of where you are right now, whether your motivation for losing weight is high or low, we will help you develop an eating style that works for you.

Do You Really Want to Change Your Eating Habits?

In our work as doctors over the years, we have seen many patients come in with a desire to lose weight but not actually implement any positive changes in their eating habits or lifestyle. These patients get frustrated, feel helpless, and move on. Sadly, many of them gain back the weight they lost within a matter of months.

We have also seen many patients share their commitment to making positive lifestyle changes.

These patients are the ones who make lasting changes in their eating habits and overall health. The bottom line is that if you are going to lose weight and keep it off for good, it takes more than just a desire for change or willpower—you must possess a willingness to transform your lifestyle over time.

The 3-Week Diet: Your Lifestyle Transformation Starts Now

"There is no such thing as instant gratification in the world of dieting and exercise." —Dr. Wayne W. Dyer.

If you're like most people, you have tried to lose weight in the past. Maybe a friend or family member has told you that a new diet might be just what you need to lose those last 10 pounds. Or maybe you've read a book that promises permanent weight loss in 14 days (or even less!). What we want you to know is that although what you are about to read will make a difference, it won't happen overnight. If you are looking for an easy way out, think again.

We're sorry if we sound a little pessimistic here, but we want you to understand that although this program is very different from other fad diets, the "3-Week Diet" does offer permanent weight loss if you follow the plan long term. We have been asked before why we don't just tell everyone there is a magic bullet for weight loss—an "easy way out." Simply because there is no "easy way out." The only way to lose weight, keep it off and stay healthy is to consistently implement the five components of our program over time.

The good news is that we are going to show you how to do this in just three weeks. If you follow the plan we lay out in this book, you will lose anywhere from 5-10 pounds (or more!). This program works for a very specific reason—it helps you develop a lifestyle that supports your weight loss efforts. By the end of the three weeks, you will have laid the groundwork for a lifetime of successful weight maintenance.

There are two things we'd like you to have in mind as you read this book. First, this book has been designed for people who are serious about losing weight and keeping it off long term. We know that many diet books give "tips" for losing weight without any explanation of how those tips fit in with the rest of your life. Our approach is different; we believe that it is important to teach you how to implement sustainable lifestyle changes that will support your weight loss efforts over time.

Chapter 8: Common Issues In Nutrition and Fitness (Part I) - Motivational Interviewing.

It is no secret that the number of people with serious health conditions is increasing. And while this may be a challenge for the medical and pharmaceutical industries, it has not been difficult to find support from research, nutritionists, fitness coaches, dieticians and advisors on how to prevent these diseases from occurring or at least delay their onset.

The question then becomes one about how to help someone who is developing or experiencing these diseases and how to motivate them -- which brings us back nicely to Motivational Interviewing.

As we have discussed before, Motivational Interviewing is a technique for helping individuals make and maintain changes in behaviour important to them. It is typically done in conjunction with another technique (which we will discuss later), but unlike the latter, it also focuses on the client/patient's views about their problems and behaviours. In other words, it tries to understand why they are changing or not changing, what it will take for them to change and how they can handle different barriers they may face.

The application of Motivational Interviewing to the field of nutrition and fitness have been tested in multiple trials, with good results. For example, a study by MacHovec et al (2011) found that usage of Motivational Interviewing techniques greatly enhanced dietary improvements in obese women going through an 8-week training program. Another study by Strauss et al. (2013) on morbidly obese patients undergoing bariatric surgery found that nutritional pre-habilitation could be improved significantly using the Motivational Interviewing. A study by Cottler et al. (2009) also tested the use of Motivational Interviewing in an adolescent obesity clinic, with good results.

Studies that have looked into self-reported usage of Motivational Interviewing in the field of nutrition and fitness have also reported favourable results. For example, a study by Heiwe et al. (2006) found that nurses who were trained to use Motivational Interviewing techniques for their patients achieved better results than those who did not use it.

Many other studies have been conducted demonstrating the advantages of using Motivational Interviewing in conjunction with various diets and training programs to improve success rates, both in terms of patient satisfaction and ongoing behaviour changes after the program comes to a conclusion.

All in all, with the impressive body of research that has been done to date, it is beyond dispute that Motivational Interviewing is a technique that deserves more attention and use by fitness professionals and nutritionists. It has by no means replaced other diet/health/exercise programs or techniques, but its use should become more widespread nonetheless.

Common Issues In Nutrition and Fitness (Part II) - The Relationship Of Nutrition And Exercise To Health and Disease

With the role of diet in weight loss being such a hot topic, many people are looking for answers as to how diet impacts health. The truth is that there are many ways in which diet can impact your health, some of them good and some not so good. There is a vast amount of research on this topic, but this book will focus on some of the most common issues related to the impact of nutrition on health.

1) Weight Gain/Obesity: One of the most well known ways that nutrition impacts your health revolves around weight gain or obesity. A poor diet is the main cause of obesity and other weight related diseases. A large number of studies have demonstrated the close connection between diet and weight, with results showing that nutrition

has a direct impact on fat oxidation, fat storage and other factors that affect how much fat you gain versus how much you lose.

2) Energy Drinks/Supplements: Another common issue related to nutrition and health revolves around energy drinks and supplements. These types of products are usually very heavily marketed, with claims about their benefit to your workout habits or general health. However, many people do not know the negative aspects of these products and in some cases they can be dangerous if used incorrectly. For example, caffeine is often found in energy drinks and is well known for increasing your heart rate and energy. However, some people can actually suffer from caffeine overdose if they do not use it in moderation, which can lead to serious health problems.

It is important to note that many of the stimulants used in energy drinks and supplements are illegal to use without a prescription and should only be acquired from professionals when necessary. It's also important that people looking for an energy boost during their workout adhere to their trainer's instructions on the proper dosage of these products. Not doing so could result in serious health problems or even death.

3) Diabetes: Another serious disease related to nutrition is diabetes. It's estimated that over 25.8 million people have diabetes in the United States alone and it is often a very serious disease because of the complications it can cause to other organs in the body. A number of factors contribute to diabetes, but genetics are a large factor with type 1 diabetes being an autoimmune disorder and type 2 diabetes being directly related to obesity and physical inactivity. This has led many researchers to believe that nutrition is a major factor for not only preventing diabetes, but also treating it once you develop symptoms.

4) Heart Disease: Heart disease is another well known risk of poor diet and lack of exercise. As mentioned earlier, one of the major causes of heart disease is obesity. It's estimated that over 50% of people who die from heart disease are also obese. Additionally, many studies show a direct correlation between the amount of meat and saturated fats you consume and the risk of

developing heart disease. All in all, nutrition plays a significant role in the overall health of your cardiovascular system, which is why it is so important to focus on a healthy diet if you suffer from any type of heart condition.

5) Inflammation/Autoimmune Disorders: One more issue directly related to diet and health is inflammation or autoimmune disorders. Many people associate inflammation with allergies, but it can also be caused by many other factors including poor diet and exercise. For example, a poor diet is often cited as one of the causes of autoimmune disorders such as lupus, rheumatoid arthritis and multiple sclerosis. Additionally it's estimated that nearly 70% of people with an autoimmune disorder are also overweight or obese.

Lifestyle Choices & The Effect on Health

As you can see, nutrition has many positive aspects to it that help you improve your health when done correctly. However, just like anything else in life, choosing healthy foods can be very difficult if you do not have the right tools or support available to you. If you are looking for ways to improve the overall health and wellness of your life, it may be helpful to begin with analyzing your current daily routine and habits.

Here are a few common lifestyle choices that can be improved upon to overall improve your health:

Exercise: Physical inactivity is one of the main contributors to many diseases and poor physical health. In fact, it is estimated that more than 30% of American adults do not exercise on a regular basis. If this describes you, consider making the decision today that you will begin exercising on a regular basis. You can start out small by walking on a nightly walk or adding some strength training exercises into your weekly routine.

Physical inactivity is one of the main contributors to many diseases and poor physical health. In fact, it is estimated that more than 30% of American adults do not exercise on a regular basis. If this describes you, consider making the decision today that you will begin exercising on a regular basis. You can start out small by walking on a nightly walk or adding some strength training exercises into your weekly routine. Sleep:

Lack of sleep is also a major contributor to many health issues including cardiovascular disease, diabetes and obesity to name a few. Many people have trouble sleeping consistently due to stress and anxiety issues which can also contribute to issues such as heart disease and diabetes. If you are having trouble sleeping, consider supplementing your current regiment with natural remedies that can help you get a good nights' rest such as essential oils, relaxation exercises and diffusing lavender.

Lack of sleep is also a major contributor to many health issues including cardiovascular disease, diabetes and obesity to name a few. Many people have trouble sleeping consistently due to stress and anxiety issues which can also contribute to issues such as heart disease and diabetes. If you are having trouble sleeping, consider supplementing your current regiment with natural remedies that can help you get a good nights' rest such as essential oils, relaxation exercises and diffusing lavender. I like to use this spa scented lavender oils set to help me relax at night or if you are looking for a more affordable option, just buy pure lavender essential oil. These are my favourite essential oils and you can grab them here.

The nutritional benefits of omega-3s include reducing heart disease and stroke while also helping prevent cognitive decline. If you want to incorporate omega-3s into your diet, I recommend eating 2 servings of fatty fish per week (wild-caught is best). If you don't like fish, take a high quality fish oil supplement.

6) Infections: The next issue is infections and the role nutrition plays in them. A number of infections can develop if you do not take care of your body properly. For example, if you are sick for an extended period of time it can be difficult to digest food properly and this can decrease your nutrition levels and make it more difficult to fight sickness. If you are sick for an extended period of time, focus on getting better rather than worrying about weight loss or exercising. Once you get better, then you can begin focusing on a healthy diet again.

As you can see, there are many issues related to nutrition and health which makes it a critical part of maintaining wellness or preventing disease. If you are looking for additional information about nutrition, be sure to check out my book on the top 10 nutrients for health.

Common Issues In Nutrition and Fitness (Part 1) - The Role of Diet and Exercise in Health and Disease

Just like any other field, the field of nutrition has many questions that people are constantly trying to answer about how diet and exercise affect your health. While many fitness professionals, nutritionists and dieticians can explain the basics about how it works, there are a lot of common misconceptions about this topic which may prevent people from making the right decisions for their health. In this book we will be addressing many issues related to diet and exercise including both the truths and myths behind them.

Chapter 9: New Developments in Nutrition and Fitness

Motivational Interviewing in Nutrition and Fitness: The Proven Consulting Approach to Help Clients Overcome Ambivalence, Break Free from Diets and Overcome Barriers to Change

The field of health and fitness has evolved dramatically over the past decade, and new research findings continually change the way professionals approach their work. In this chapter we highlight recent developments in the field that have a direct bearing on nutrition and fitness, and we include examples of how motivational interviewing can be applied in each case. There will always be a place for the tried-and-true methods of nutrition and physical activity, but as new findings emerge it is incumbent on health and fitness professionals to make efforts to stay abreast of these developments.

Research Findings that Have a Direct Bearing on Nutrition and Fitness

1. Knowledge is not power.

Research shows that people who are knowledgeable about nutrition and health are no more likely to change their behaviour than those who know little about the subject. With this knowledge, health professionals and consumers alike have a new challenge: recognizing that knowledge alone does not lead to behaviour change and that additional strategies must be employed.

Research shows that people who are knowledgeable about nutrition and health are no more likely to change their behaviour than those who know little about the subject. What is even more interesting is that research shows that people who are knowledgeable about nutrition and health don't believe they need to change certain behaviours . The study of many different types of knowledge, from IQ to financial literacy, has revealed something very important: knowledge does not equal power. Knowing about a subject does not necessarily mean you have the skills needed to execute the knowledge and do what is necessary.

2. Cognitive restraint is related to disordered eating.

People with a tendency toward disordered eating often use strategies such as cognitive restraint, which involves using willpower to avoid thinking about food in order to reduce its appeal and consumption. This is so common that the practice has been given its own name: "restraint-based dieting." Unfortunately it doesn't work (de Luca et al. , 2010).

A growing body of research indicates that dieting leads to disordered eating . Research has revealed one particularly important trait in those with a history of disordered eating. People who use cognitive restraint are less likely to lose weight and maintain their weight loss than those who don't. When people try to be extremely mindful about food, they often find it difficult not to think about forbidden foods. Their effort at restraint makes them feel bad (de Luca et al., 2010).

The same principle is true for physical activity. Pushing yourself to exercise after a long day at work is likely to leave you feeling overexerted and more fatigued the next day when you are already pressed for time. In both cases, it is better to schedule exercise into your routine so it becomes part of a natural pattern, rather than trying to force yourself to engage in activity you don't feel ready for.

3. The research on willpower and self-control shows that people have a limited amount.

People have the same amount of willpower and self-control as they have buckets. Over time, if one bucket is emptied people will use up more than their supply of willpower to fill it up again, making themselves susceptible to temptation in the future. As a result, all sorts of bad behaviour is more likely when a person exceeds his or her limit (Baumeister et al., 2003).

One of the most important research findings for health and fitness professionals, and for all people interested in maintaining their health and fitness, is that there is a limited amount of self-control or willpower available in each day. Evidence suggests that there are two types of self-control: one involving the brain (controlled by the prefrontal cortex) and one involving hormones (controlled by the limbic system). There is evidence that the amount of self-control available each day depends on the balance between these two. As a result, any time people use self-control they deplete their supply, making them more likely to give in to temptation in the future. They become much more prone to acting impulsively (Baumeister et al., 2003; Muraven et al., 2006; Vohs et al., 2006).

4. Exercise enhances brain plasticity.

Research on animal models and limited research on humans has revealed that exercise enhances brain plasticity, which has important implications for brain injury.

Research shows that exercise enhanced the ability of animal models to grow new neurons in their brains. In recent years, research has found that exercise enhances brain plasticity or the ability of nerve cells to grow to different areas of the brain and form new connections. This is dependent upon an enzyme called CREB (transcription factor). Studies have found that CREB is necessary for the promotion of new neuron growth, or neurogenesis (Gould et al., 1999).

Research has also found that exercise increases the number of synapses in certain areas of certain brains, such as those of animals with brain injuries. As a result, physical activity may enhance recovery after brain injury in these cases (Gomez-Pinilla et al., 2008) .

5. Exercise improves self-control and mental focus.

A growing body of research shows that exercise is effective in increasing self-control and improving mental focus. These are critical for success in school and careers, but can also be key to maintaining health and fitness.

In one set of studies researchers found that exercise reduced the ability to maintain focus on a particular task (Casey et al., 2007). This may seem like a disadvantage, but alternative research found that people who exercised could more effectively switch between tasks than those who did not (Prakash et al., 2009).

Research found that physical activity enhances the ability to delay gratification. In one study, children who played outside on a regular basis were better able to wait than those who did not (McCoy et al., 2007).

The ability of exercise to increase self-control and mental focus is also important for people with attention-deficit/hyperactivity disorder (ADHD) (Sugawara et al., 2010).

6. Exercise improves memory.

Work in animals has shown that exercise can enhance memory and learning. While this has not been as well documented in humans, there is some evidence that exercise can enhance memory and learning in people.

Work with animals has shown a clear link between exercise and the ability to learn and remember. Studies have found that physical activity can help improve memory and learning through several different mechanisms (Sweat et al., 2008). In one study, researchers found that exercise helped increase the number of connections between neurons in the brain involved in long-term memory (Tanapat et al., 1999). This helped rats remember how to navigate a maze over time.

Research with humans has also found that exercise can help improve memory. In a set of studies, researchers found that aerobic activity helped improve spatial memory. They also found that exercise can help improve working memory (Borst et al., 2010).

This is an important advantage for students and those in careers that require effortful concentration and mental focus, like medical school or the law. Exercise may also help people with conditions like Alzheimer's disease or other types of dementia (Cotman et al. 2000).

7. Exercise can help people manage stress and anxiety.

Physical activity helps release endorphins, which are natural feel-good chemicals in the body that can help relieve stress (Raab et al., 2010). This is important because chronic stress is a risk factor for many illnesses and conditions, including heart disease, diabetes, and depression. Exercise may also reduce the level of cortisol in the body (Kamijo et al., 2005). This is a risk factor for developing heart disease. It can also help people sleep better and feel less anxious (Orr, 2009). All of these are important benefits for students who are preparing to take exams.

8. Exercise can help improve blood sugar control in those with diabetes.

Physical activity helps reduce the risk of developing type 2 diabetes (Couch et al., 2013). Exercise can also help those with diabetes manage their blood sugar levels and prevent complications, such as heart disease and stroke (Campbell et al., 2011).

9. Exercise can improve academic performance.

Students who exercise do academically better than those who don't (Cohen et al., 2012; Joosen & Wiersma, 2011; Raab et al., 2010; Thompson & Sherman, 2011; Weinberg & Gould, 2012). Several studies have found that exercise helps improve alertness, attention, and concentration (Dishman 2006). According to the American Psychological Association, "Kids who are fit may perform better in school and have higher grades because of their greater ability to focus and concentrate" (Dishman 2006). Exercise can also help students make friends more easily. These characteristics make exercise a valuable tool to help students grow socially, mentally, emotionally, and academically (Cohen et al., 2012; Joosen & Wiersma, 2011; Raab et al., 2010).

10. Exercise improves self-esteem.

11. Exercise improves sleep.

12. Exercise improves sexual activity.

13. Exercise increases energy levels and stamina.

Chapter 10: Common Issues In Nutrition and Fitness (Part II) - Motivational Interviewing

Motivational Interviewing is the use of active, non-judgmental questions in a conversation with a clinician to help clients overcome ambivalence, break free from diets and overcome barriers to change. The goal of this form of therapy is increased intrinsic motivation and readiness for change. According to Miller, Rollick and Butler (2013), the patients and clinicians are in a consultation relationship built on respect, trust and empathy. The clinician attempts to:

Motivational Interviewing (MI) is a form of therapy that uses the client, their inherent motivation, and their readiness to make needed changes in behaviour. This therapy does not focus on behaviour change per se; instead it focuses on changing the relationship between the client and their thoughts about physical activity or fitness. The goal is to get the client to think more positively about their current behaviour, or to develop new thoughts and feelings that would lead them to act in a way that is consistent with their needs.

Therefore, the clinician focuses on building a collaborative relationship with the client in order to identify and change beliefs which are barriers to optimal health-related behaviours. The essence of MI is the "collaborative management of meaning," in which clients are empowered and encouraged towards autonomy within an empowering relationship (Miller et al., 2013). This facilitative process is grounded in the belief that both clinicians and clients are self-determined, self-motivated, and inherently capable of change, even if they have been unsuccessful in the past

(Miller et al., 2013). The skills used by MI include clarification questions, reflective listening, summarizing, and encouraging of client action. The skilled clinician uses these skills to help clients explore their thoughts and feelings about physical activity or fitness. These skills are used to build rapport and trust, and to explore the client's beliefs.

MI is used in all settings, including medical clinics, community-based programs, schools and workplaces (Miller et al., 2013). Use of this approach in nutrition and fitness is based upon the theory that health professionals can influence patients' readiness for behaviour change by providing supportive encouragement and reframing of their thoughts about physical activity or fitness. As noted above, MI does not focus on behaviour change per se.

Regarding the specific content of MI, health professionals may help clients develop insight about when, how, and why they engage in target behaviours (McCrady et al., 1995). In addition to teaching clients specific skills for increasing intrinsic motivation and self-efficacy, clinicians can also provide information about their target behaviour. MI is also an appropriate approach for working with diverse populations. It is suggested that doctors use MI with ethnic minority patients due to cultural considerations when identifying helpful interventions. It is important for doctors to take into account the fact that some minority groups may more strongly believe in the concept of fate or destiny rather than control over their own lives (Tate, McPherson, & Simonson, 2003). This is relevant to when people are identifying barriers and developing their LSMWT.

Overall, MI has been found to be effective across several medical and health settings for increasing physical activity (Foster et al., 2007; Tate et al., 2003). MI has also been effective for increasing physical activity in individuals with heart disease or coronary artery disease (Foster et al., 2007). Following MI counselling, these patients reported better enjoyment of exercise and more vigorous physical activity. MI strategies such as motivational interviewing have been suggested to be useful in cancer prevention (Harpaz-Rotem, Ratzoni, & Shoham, 2006). Medical settings have included the use of motivational interviewing for cessation of smoking (Foster et al., 2007. MI is effective in substance abuse setting as well. One study looked at the effects of motivational interviewing in an attempt to decrease the participants alcohol intake (Davison, Tannenbaum & Kokotailo, 2007). Results indicated that MI was effective at reducing alcohol intake over time.

A common barrier in using MI with fitness clients is that, for many people, physical activity or fitness is a choice motivated by perceived negative consequences of not engaging in it. One can evaluate the perceived risk of not engaging in physical activity or fitness by means of proper assessment. The following steps to use MI with clients are:

In a study by Schinke, Kristeller, and Brown (2013), it was found that individuals who were treated with MI were more likely to continue their daily fitness routine after the program ended than non-treated participants. Results from this study showed that MI was effective at improving physical activity and fitness, even after the completion of the program.

Motivational interviewing has been used in different stages of care to improve health behaviours. Motivational interviewing was applied to help patients with type 2 diabetes (T2D) be more compliant with medical treatment. A study of thirty patients indicated that motivational interviewing was successful in improving patient self-care behaviours when compared to a control group (Booth et al., 2009). The study included health professionals with a degree in nursing or health sciences. The results of the study showed that patients who received motivational interviewing were more likely to have a decrease in A1C, less likely to have an increase in systolic and diastolic blood pressure, and also had a decrease in medication use compared to the control group. This shows that MI was successful at improving patient compliance with their medical treatment and improving their overall health.

The same study also proved that motivational interviewing was successful at treating patients who had T2D and were overweight or obese. A study of thirty-six overweight or obese patients with T2D showed that health professionals with training in motivational interviewing could successfully improve weight reduction, waist circumference reduction, physical activity level, and glycolic control (McCrady et al., 2007). All of these health behaviors are positively associated with increased longevity in patients.

In another study to determine the effectiveness of motivational interviewing in improving overall health behaviour, a team of researchers decided to target HIV/AIDS patients. The results of this study showed that motivational interviewing could be an effective way to improve the quality of life of these patients (Campbell & Hogg, 2009). Overall, this study concluded that MI was successful at improving health behaviours for people with T2D and HIV/AIDS.

Motivational interviewing is a method that can be used in many different stages of care. In the treatment of chronic illness, motivational interviewing has been used to improve compliance through treatment and to lead to better outcomes for the patient. MI was successful at improving health behaviours for HIV/AIDS patients and T2D patients.

Although MI seems effective in changing attitudes, intentions, self-efficacy, and behaviours in many different cases, one study actually reported a negative effect on participants. In this study, the researchers sought to prove MI was successful in changing behaviour, and that participants who underwent motivational interviewing were more likely to use condoms during sexual intercourse. However, the study actually found that participants who went through motivational interviewing were less likely to use condoms during sexual intercourse (Thompson et al., 2013). The results of this study varied from what has been reported in other studies of MI, which may be due to different length and format of interviews and different types of participants.

Motivational interviewing is not commonly used in mental health settings, but it appears to be an effective way to change attitudes and behaviours of patients. MI has been successful at changing behaviours for HIV/AIDS patients, T2D patients, and smokers; however, one study found a negative effect with MI. Motivational interviewing seems effective in changing attitudes, intentions, self-efficacy, and behaviours in many different cases.

Chapter 11: Issues With Motivational Interviewing in Nutrition and Fitness

Motivational interviewing in nutrition and fitness is a proven approach to help people who are ambivalent about changing their diet or increasing their activity levels.

A client's motivation can be low for many reasons, including the following:

- Lack of knowledge about how to make changes in nutrition and exercise.

- Barriers such as lack of time, cost, or fear of discomfort associated with changing from a more sedentary lifestyle to an active one.

- Lack of willpower to make changes.

- An immediate need to change, but lack of motivation to follow through over time.

- Fear of failure.

- The belief that it's too late to make a difference in health and fitness, even when there is still time left to do so.

- The belief that it's too hard or impossible to change eating habits and activity patterns.

- Fear of losing control.

- Fear of making a mistake.

- A lack of encouragement to change.

People are often motivated to change before a crisis occurs, but once they are in the thick of it — in the middle of an acute health condition such as diabetes or heart disease — they become less motivated and more discouraged and anxious about their situation. It's hard not to feel overwhelmed by the sense that it's too late for you and that no one will help you.

Many people who are chronically ill become discouraged about their health and lose motivation. A dietician can't change a client's disease, but the client may feel that he or she has to try anyway—and when the client gets discouraged about failing, it reinforces the sense of hopelessness. The depression that often accompanies chronic illness can be devastating, but dieticians can help clients manage it so that they don't become totally sedentary and despairing.

It's important for dieticians to understand their own feelings about helping clients change by looking at what they believe is possible and how much effort they are willing to put in before clients hit a crisis. Working with a client who is already struggling can be emotionally draining, and dieticians may have to set limits on how far they are willing to go as a service provider.

Motivational interviewing (MI) is a collaborative, client-cantered process that can help individuals move from where they are to where they want to be.

Motivational interviewing was developed from the principles of reflective listening by psychologists James Prochaska and Carlo DiClemente. They found that the way to help a client change is not to tell him or her what the problem is but to ask the client about his or her experience and try to understand it from that perspective. This approach empowers clients to see themselves as capable of initiating and maintaining changes in their life circumstances.

The goal of motivational interviewing is to help clients explore their own readiness to change by exploring ambivalence about whether or not they really want to change. The process of motivational interviewing helps clients to a) identify their own barriers to change, b) engage in values-based decision making, and c) set goals based on their own self-determined agenda. The active participation of the client is a critical component of this approach.

Motivational interviewing helps people understand that they are ambivalent about changing by revealing the messages that they have told themselves about not changing and by helping them see how those messages have been barriers to change. It is very therapeutic to help someone see how irrational and destructive their core beliefs about change have been.

Core Beliefs About Change (CBC) can be identified easily in a nutritional assessment, and it can be helpful to structure the intake interview around your knowledge of the client's CBCs.

The core beliefs of a client may include any of the following:

- There is no point in trying to make changes because it's too late for me.

- It's impossible to make changes.

- I'm powerless to make changes in my diet and physical activity.

- I don't have enough discipline to change.

- I'll gain weight if I give up (food, alcohol, cigarettes, etc.).

- It's impossible to eat well on a budget.

- If I change the way I eat, people will reject me or think less of me.

- If I start exercising, I'll hurt myself or burn out or get discouraged.

- I don't have time to make changes.

- It's too much effort to make changes.

- It would be too embarrassing for me to ask others for help — or it would be insulting to talk with others about my problems.

There are two skills needed in motivational interviewing: **reflective listening** and **questioning skills.**

Reflective listening means paraphrasing what the client has said using her own words and offering behaviours only to a very small degree. A question intended to open dialogue is called an open-ended question, whereas a question used to gather information is called a closed-ended question.

Open-ended questions are the most useful in motivational interviewing because they encourage clients to describe their own experience of change or lack of change, rather than forcing them into categories that may not apply to them.

Questions should be brief, open-ended, and simple so that clients do not feel overwhelmed by information. It is important to note whether clients are flowing rather than making pauses while talking—it is typical for them to pause while they reflect on what they have said and decide how much more of their story to tell you.

Questions should be specific, not hypothetical, and the answer to the question should be clear.

Here are some questions that can be helpful in motivational interviewing:

- What was it like (today, this morning) to eat breakfast? Just tell me what you did.

- What was it like to eat lunch?

- Did you notice any differences between yesterday and today, or between this morning and this afternoon?

- How did you feel about the changes you have made?

- What else do you think affected how you ate (today or this week)?

- If a friend asked you for help, what would you say to him/her?

- What are some of the advantages you have noticed from eating this way?

- When do you think it's a good idea to eat something sweet? When is it not so good to have sweets?

- How did you feel after having that dessert today?

- What might happen if you didn't eat the dessert today?

Motivational interviewing (MI) has been applied in many domains, including alcohol and other drug use disorder treatment, asthma and diabetes care, and weight management. Other behavioural health areas such as depression, anxiety disorders, bipolar disorder, psychosis and schizophrenia can be helped with motivational interviewing. Smoking cessation treatments that include motivational interviewing are often more effective than those that don't. MI has also proven useful in patient-provider interactions for vulnerable children and adolescents. It has been applied to a wide range of medical conditions, such as heart failure, hypertension, asthma, trauma rehabilitation, chronic obstructive pulmonary disease (COPD), cancer treatment, diabetes care, sexual health education and risk reduction for sexually transmitted infections (STIs), and pain management. Long-acting reversible contraception (LARC) can be promoted to teenage girls with motivational interviewing techniques. In fact, motivational interviewing is one of the methods used in FAMILAC community interventions (Familial Approach to Mental Illness and Alcoholism Care).

Motivational interviewing is used as a primary method for treating tobacco dependence in federally-funded behavioural health and primary care settings. A meta-analysis of randomized controlled trials found MI to be the most effective treatment of tobacco dependence relative to other interventions, including nicotine replacement therapy (NRT). Motivational interviewing has been found to increase cessation rates by approximately 50% more than NRT. In combination with NRT, motivational interviewing was shown to increase cessation up to a total of 73%.

Behavioural adolescents who received motivational interviewing training in primary care had fewer diagnosed STIs, compared with adolescents who did not receive the same training.

The parents of children receiving motivational interviewing in a paediatric obesity clinic were less likely to perceive their child's weight as a result of poor diet and lack of activity, compared to parents who received care as usual.

Motivational interviewing has been used to help people with problems such as cardiovascular disease, asthma, alcohol dependence, cocaine dependence, and mental illness. Research is underway to evaluate the effectiveness of MI for enhancing adherence to antiretroviral therapy in HIV-infected injection drug users; for decreasing alcohol consumption; for preventing postpartum depression; and in adolescent counselling. A meta-analysis by Humphreys and colleagues found MI was moderately effective against substance abuse and behavioural addictions including gambling disorder and sexual addiction.

Conclusion

Motivational Interviewing is a powerful counselling approach that empowers clients to make changes and overcome barriers to change. It accomplishes this without shaming, blaming, or coercing the individual. Rather, it provides support and empathy within a non-judgmental environment in which the client sets goals collaboratively with the counsellor as opposed to receiving commands from them. When used with nutrition and fitness clients, motivational interviewing addresses ambivalence about making changes, resolves conflicts about dieting versus changing eating behaviours in more general ways, and helps clients work through barriers that impede change.

And now for my favourite part: how you can incorporate motivational interviewing into your consulting work!

1) Engage in Rapport Building (building trust).

This is crucial for any type of counselling to be successful.

2) Ask Questions, Set the Agenda (Clarifying the problem and setting goals).

Use open-ended questions, and terms such as "what", "how", and "why". Also, use reflective listening by restating what the client has said in your own words to show both that you heard them and that you are actively listening. This will also help clarify the client's perspectives.

3) Empower Clients by Restoring a Sense of Choice & Control.

Creating a sense of choice is valuable because internal locus of control can strongly influence motivation and self-efficacy to pursue change as well as the likelihood of success during intervention.

4) Help Clients Address Any Conflicts About Change

One technique for addressing ambivalence is to help the client identify their reasons for change and reasons for staying the same. This will help the client figure out which reasons are more dominant. If reasoning and ambivalence are equal, then you may need to offer additional support or suggestions. If one side is stronger than the other, then you can use that to motivate change.

5) Facilitate Coping Skills

Another technique is to investigate how clients have tried to deal with their eating issues in the past. This can help them figure out which coping skills are helpful and which ones aren't. Once they know which skills are helpful, you can teach them new strategies that will help them in the future.

6) Provide Support

It's important to provide support and empathy to clients while maintaining a non-judgmental stance. Providing support without judgment is crucial when your client is suffering from an eating disorder or is otherwise mentally ill.

7) Explore and Identify Barriers to Change

Finally, the best thing you can do for your clients is help them identify barriers to change so that they can develop a plan of action for overcoming these obstacles.